# Problem Solving and Reasoning Pupil Book 6

Peter Clarke

William Collins' dream of knowledge for all began with the publication of his first book in 1819. A self-educated mill worker, he not only enriched millions of lives, but also founded a flourishing publishing house. Today, staying true to this spirit, Collins books are packed with inspiration, innovation and practical expertise. They place you at the centre of a world of possibility and give you exactly what you need to explore it.

Collins. Freedom to teach.

Published by Collins
An imprint of HarperCollins*Publishers*
The News Building
1 London Bridge Street
London
SE1 9GF

Browse the complete Collins catalogue at
**www.collins.co.uk**

© HarperCollins*Publishers* Limited 2018

10 9 8 7 6 5 4 3 2 1

ISBN 978-0-00-826051-4

The author wishes to thank Brian Molyneaux for his valuable contribution to this publication.

British Library Cataloguing in Publication Data
A Catalogue record for this publication is available from the British Library

Author: Peter Clarke
Publishing manager: Fiona McGlade
Editor: Amy Wright
Copyeditor: Catherine Dakin
Proofreader: Tanya Solomons
Answer checker: Steven Matchett
Cover designer: Amparo Barrera
Internal designer: 2hoots Publishing Services
Typesetter: Ken Vail Graphic Design
Illustrator: Eva Sassin
Production controller: Sarah Burke
Printed and bound by Martins the Printers

MIX
Paper from
responsible sources
FSC™ C007454

# Contents

Using and applying mathematics in real-world contexts

# How to use this book

## Aims

This book aims to provide teachers with a resource that enables pupils to:

- develop mathematical problem solving and thinking skills
- reason and communicate mathematically
- use and apply mathematics to solve problems.

## The three different types of mathematical problem solving challenge

This book consists of three different types of mathematical problem solving challenge:

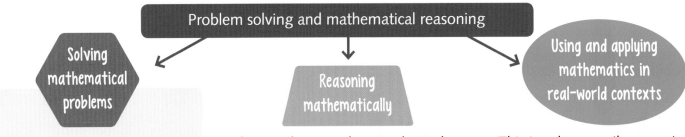

This involves pupils investigating, exploring and applying their mathematical knowledge and skills to solve problems 'within' mathematics itself.

This involves pupils using logical thinking to solve problems, focusing on making conjectures and generalisations, and explaining and justifying conclusions using appropriate language.

This involves pupils engaging in challenges that require them to use and apply their mathematical knowledge and skills in open-ended, real-world contexts.

This book is intended as a 'dip-in' resource, where teachers choose which of the three different types of challenge they wish pupils to undertake. A challenge may form the basis of part of or an entire mathematics lesson. The challenges can also be used in a similar way to the weekly bank of 'Learning activities' found in the *Busy Ant Maths* Teacher's Guide. It is recommended that pupils have equal experience of all three types of challenge during the course of a term.

The 'Solving mathematical problems' and 'Reasoning mathematically' challenges are organised under the different topics (domains) of the 2014 National Curriculum for Mathematics. This is to make it easier for teachers to choose a challenge that corresponds to the topic they are currently teaching, thereby providing an opportunity for pupils to practise their pure mathematical knowledge and skills in a problem solving context. These challenges are designed to be completed during the course of a lesson.

The 'Using and applying mathematics in real-world contexts' challenges have not been organised by topic. The very nature of this type of challenge means that pupils are drawing on their mathematical knowledge and skills from several topics in order to investigate challenges arising from the real world. In many cases these challenges will require pupils to work on them for an extended period, such as over the course of several lessons, a week or during a particular unit of work. An indication of which topics each of these challenges covers can be found on page 5.

# Briefing

As with other similar teaching and learning resources, pupils will engage more fully with each challenge if the teacher introduces and discusses the challenge with the pupils. This includes reading through the challenge with the pupils, checking prerequisites for learning, ensuring understanding and clarifying any misconceptions.

# Working collaboratively

The challenges can be undertaken by individuals, pairs or groups of pupils, however they will be enhanced greatly if pupils are able to work together in pairs or groups. By working collaboratively, pupils are more likely to develop their problem solving, communicating and reasoning skills.

# You will need

All of the challenges require pupils to use pencil and paper. Giving pupils a large sheet of paper, such as A3 or A2, allows them to feel free to work out the results and record their thinking in ways that are appropriate to them. It also enables pupils to work together better in pairs or as a group, and provides them with an excellent prompt to use when sharing and discussing their work with others.

An important problem solving skill is to be able to identify not only the mathematics, but also what resources to use. For this reason, many of the challenges do not name the specific resources that are needed.

# Characters

The characters on the right are the teacher and the four children who appear in some of the challenges in this book.

Ms Moore

Sofia

Eve

Johannes

David

# Think about ...

All challenges include prompting questions that provide both a springboard and a means of assisting pupils in accessing and working through the challenge.

# What if?

The challenges also include an extension or variation that allows pupils to think more deeply about the challenge and to further develop their thinking skills.

# When you've finished, ...

At the bottom of each challenge, pupils are instructed to turn to page 80 and to find a partner or another pair or group. This page offers a structure and set of questions intended to provide pupils with an opportunity to share their results and discuss their methods, strategies and mathematical reasoning.

When you've finished, turn to page 80.

# Solutions

Where appropriate, the solutions to the challenges in this book can be found at *Busy Ant Maths* on Collins Connect and on our website: collins.co.uk/busyantmaths.

## Challenge

Shuffle a set of 1–9 digit cards. Choose the top four cards.

| | 4 | 7 | 2 | 9 |

**You will need:**
• set of 1–9 digit cards

Use these cards to make different 2-, 3- and 4-digit numbers.

Then round each:

• 2-digit number to the nearest ten
• 3-digit number to the nearest ten and hundred
• 4-digit number to the nearest ten, hundred and thousand.

## Think about ...

For the 'Challenge', make sure that you use the four digit cards to create at least six 2-digit numbers, six 3-digit numbers and six 4-digit numbers.

For the 'What if?', make sure that you use the four digit cards to create at least three decimals with 1 decimal place (tenths), three decimals with 2 decimal places (hundredths), and three decimals with 3 decimal places (thousandths).

## What if?

What if you use the four digit cards to make different decimal numbers for tenths, hundredths and thousandths?

Multiply each of the decimal numbers by 10, 100 and 1000.

Divide each tenth by 10 and 100, and each hundredth by 10.

Round each decimal with:

• 1 decimal place to the nearest whole number
• 2 decimal places to the nearest tenth and whole number
• 3 decimal places to the nearest hundredth, tenth and whole number.

9·2
47·29
7·492

47·29 × 10 =
47·29 × 100 =
47·29 × 1000 =

9·2 ÷ 10 =
9·2 ÷ 100 =
47·29 ÷ 10 =

47·29
– rounded to the nearest tenth is . . .
– rounded to the nearest whole number is . . .

When you've finished, turn to page 80.

## Challenge

Spin the spinner four times. Each time, write down the number spun.

Using these four numbers, investigate how close to zero you can get using addition and/or subtraction.

Repeat using other sets of four numbers.

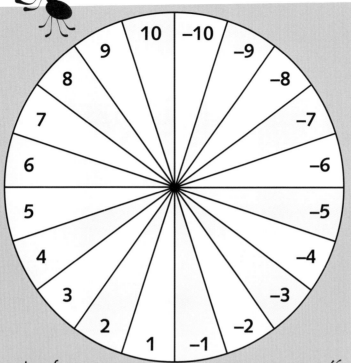

**How to use the spinner**

Hold the paper clip in the centre of the spinner using a pencil and gently flick the paper clip with your finger to make it spin.

## Think about ...

You don't have to use all four numbers.

Write down your calculations each time.

Use this number line to help you.

## What if?

What if you spin the spinner five times?

Can you make zero in more than one way using the five numbers spun?

When you've finished, turn to page 80.

## Challenge

Use all the digits 0–9 to make a calculation with an answer between 200 and 300.

Make as many different calculations as you can.

$$34 + 75 + 89 + 12 + 60 = 270$$
$$546 + 18 + 90 - 372 = 282$$
$$325{\cdot}6 + 18{\cdot}9 - 70{\cdot}4 = 274{\cdot}1$$

## Think about ...

Use estimation to help you decide how to arrange the digits.

Work out the answer to as many calculations as you can using mental strategies, making any jottings if you need to.

## What if?

What if you have to find an answer between 300 and 350?

What about between 350 and 375?

When you've finished, turn to page 80.

## Challenge

Investigate which numbers less than 100 have proper factors that are only even numbers.

Investigate which numbers less than 100 have proper factors that are only odd numbers.

| 1 | 2 | 3 | 4 | 5 | 6 | 7 | 8 | 9 | 10 |
|---|---|---|---|---|---|---|---|---|---|
| 11 | 12 | 13 | 14 | 15 | 16 | 17 | 18 | 19 | 20 |
| 21 | 22 | 23 | 24 | 25 | 26 | 27 | 28 | 29 | 30 |
| 31 | 32 | 33 | 34 | 35 | 36 | 37 | 38 | 39 | 40 |
| 41 | 42 | 43 | 44 | 45 | 46 | 47 | 48 | 49 | 50 |
| 51 | 52 | 53 | 54 | 55 | 56 | 57 | 58 | 59 | 60 |
| 61 | 62 | 63 | 64 | 65 | 66 | 67 | 68 | 69 | 70 |
| 71 | 72 | 73 | 74 | 75 | 76 | 77 | 78 | 79 | 80 |
| 81 | 82 | 83 | 84 | 85 | 86 | 87 | 88 | 89 | 90 |
| 91 | 92 | 93 | 94 | 95 | 96 | 97 | 98 | 99 | 100 |

## Think about ...

A **factor** is a whole number that divides exactly into another whole number without a remainder.

A **prime number** is a whole number greater than 1 that can't be divided by another whole number, except for itself and 1.

**Proper factors** of a number are all its factors except 1 and the number itself.

A factor of a whole number that is also a prime number is called a **prime factor**.

## What if?

20 has two prime factors: 2 and 5.

Investigate other numbers less than 100 that have two prime factors.

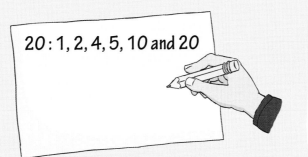

20 : 1, 2, 4, 5, 10 and 20

When you've finished, turn to page 80.

# Challenge

**5 3 1 7 2**

Shuffle a set of 0–9 digit cards.

Choose the top five cards.

Use these five digits to make a 3-digit by 2-digit multiplication calculation:

☐☐☐ × ☐☐ =

Investigate different 3-digit by 2-digit calculations using the same digits.

Which calculation gives the greatest product?

Which calculation gives the smallest product?

Can you make a calculation that gives you a product that, when rounded to the nearest 1000, rounds to 35 000?

**You will need:**
• set of 0–9 digit cards

# Think about ...

Use estimation to help you create calculations with the greatest and smallest answers and that round to the required number.

For the 'What if?' questions, think about how the inverse relationship between multiplication and division can help.

# What if?

What if you use the five cards to create a 4-digit divided by a 1-digit calculation?

☐☐☐☐ ÷ ☐ =

Which calculation gives the greatest quotient?

Which calculation gives the smallest quotient?

Can you make a calculation that gives you a quotient that, when rounded to the nearest 100, rounds to 1800?

What if you use the five cards to create a 3-digit divided by a 2-digit calculation?

☐☐☐ ÷ ☐☐ =

Which calculation gives the greatest quotient?

Which calculation gives the smallest quotient?

Can you make a calculation that gives you a quotient that, when rounded to the nearest 10, rounds to 20?

When you've finished, turn to page 80.

## Challenge

Using only the digits 1, 2, 5 and 8, investigate writing calculations that give as answers all the numbers from 0 to 10.

**1 5 2 8**

### Rules
- All four digits must be used in the calculation.
- Each digit can only be used once in each calculation.
- Digits can be joined together to form 2-digit numbers.
- Use any of the four operations: +, −, × and ÷.
- Brackets are allowed.

## Think about ...

You need to follow the order of operations: brackets then orders (or indices), followed by division and multiplication, and finally addition and subtraction.

Use known calculations for numbers to help you write calculations that give the answers to other numbers.

## What if?

What if you use the digits 1, 2, 5 and 8 to make the numbers 11 to 20?

What other whole numbers can you make?

**New rule**
2 can be used as the power of 2, that is $5^2$.

When you've finished, turn to page 80.

# Unit fractions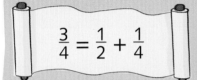

## Challenge

Apart from $\frac{2}{3}$, the Ancient Egyptians only wrote unit fractions.

This is how they might have expressed $\frac{3}{4}$ and $\frac{3}{8}$:

$$\frac{3}{4} = \frac{1}{2} + \frac{1}{4}$$

$$\frac{3}{8} = \frac{1}{4} + \frac{1}{8}$$

What non-unit fractions can you make using the Ancient Egyptian method?

## Think about ...

A unit fraction is a fraction that has 1 as its numerator, for example $\frac{1}{2}, \frac{1}{4}, \frac{1}{5}$.

Remember to add or subtract unit fractions.

A non-unit fraction is a fraction that has as its numerator any number other than 1, for example $\frac{2}{3}$, $\frac{3}{4}$ or $\frac{4}{5}$.

## What if?

How can you make the non-unit fractions you have created using the smallest possible number of fractions?

$$\frac{3}{4} = \frac{1}{2} + \frac{1}{4}$$

rather than

$$\frac{3}{4} = \frac{1}{4} + \frac{1}{4} + \frac{1}{4}$$

When you've finished, turn to page 80.

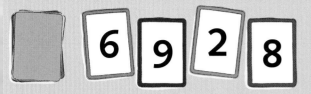

## Challenge

**You will need:**
• set of 1–9 digit cards

Shuffle a set of 1–9 digit cards.

Choose the top four cards.

Use these four digits to multiply a 1-digit number with two decimal places by a 1-digit number:

Investigate different calculations using the same digits.

Which calculation gives the greatest product?

Which calculation gives the smallest product?

Can you make a calculation that gives you a product that, when rounded to the nearest whole number, rounds to 20?

## Think about ...

Use estimation to help you create calculations with the greatest and smallest products and that round to the required whole number.

For the 'What if?', think about partitioning the 2-digit number into tens and ones. For example, $2.38 \times 47 = (2.38 \times 40) + (2.38 \times 7)$.

## What if?

What if you choose the top five cards and use the five digits to multiply a 1-digit number with 2 decimal places by a 2-digit number?

Investigate different calculations using the same digits.

Which calculation gives the greatest product?

Which calculation gives the smallest product?

Can you make a calculation that gives you a product that, when rounded to the nearest 100, rounds to 300?

When you've finished, turn to page 80.

## Challenge

**You will need:**
- calculator

$$\frac{1}{2} \quad \frac{1}{3} \quad \frac{1}{4} \quad \frac{1}{5} \quad \frac{1}{6} \quad \frac{1}{7} \quad \frac{1}{8} \quad \frac{1}{9} \quad \ldots$$

Convert some unit fractions to decimals.

Then sort the decimals into those that:

- convert to tenths
- convert to hundredths
- convert to thousandths
- are recurring decimals, for example $0 \cdot 3333\dot{3}$ or $0 \cdot 090909 \ldots$
- have anything different.

What observations and generalisations can you make?

## Think about ...

Remember, a unit fraction is a fraction that has 1 as its numerator, for example $\frac{1}{2}, \frac{1}{4}, \frac{1}{5}$.

For the 'What if?', round each percentage to the nearest whole per cent.

## What if?

For each of the unit fractions you converted to equivalent decimals in the 'Challenge', work out the equivalent percentages.

Convert some non-unit fractions such as:
$\frac{2}{3}, \frac{3}{4}, \frac{2}{5}, \frac{3}{5}, \frac{4}{5}, \frac{5}{6} \ldots$ to decimals and work out the equivalent percentages.

When you've finished, turn to page 80.

What observations and generalisations can you make?

## Challenge

0 1 2 3 4 5 6 7 8 9

**You will need:**
- set of 0–9 digit cards

How many of these percentage statements can you make using five of the 0–9 digit cards?

☐☐ % × ☐☐ = ☐

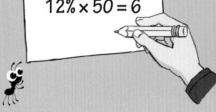

$25\% \times 16 = 4$

$12\% \times 50 = 6$

You can't use the same digit twice in a statement.

## Think about ...

Think about equivalent fractions and decimals to help you write different statements.

Start with percentages such as 10%, 20%, 25%, 50% and 75%.

## What if?

What if you use four of the 0–9 digit cards?

How many of these percentage statements can you make?

☐ % × ☐☐ = ☐

What if you use six of the 0–9 digit cards?

How many of these percentage statements can you make?

☐☐ % × ☐☐ = ☐☐

When you've finished, turn to page 80.

17

# Domino ratios

## Challenge

Look at a set of dominoes with the double blank removed,

that is:

Count the total number of dots on each domino.  3 + 6 = 9

What fraction of the dominoes have totals that are an even number?

What fraction of the dominoes have totals that are an odd number?

What is the ratio of even totals to odd totals?

## Think about ...

Be systematic in the way you record the totals, differences and products.

## What if?

Look at a set of dominoes with the doubles removed, that is:

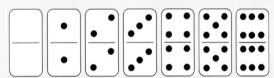

What if you find the difference between the number of dots on

each side? 6 – 3 = 3

What fraction of the dominoes have differences that are an even number?

What fraction of the dominoes have differences that are an odd number?

What is the ratio of even differences to odd differences?

Look at a set of dominoes with the dominoes with a blank removed, that is:

What if you multiply together the number of dots on each side?

3 × 6 = 18

What fraction of the dominoes have products that are an even number?

What fraction of the dominoes have products that are an odd number?

What is the ratio of even products to odd products?

When you've finished, turn to page 80.

# Algebraic expressions

## Challenge

Without substituting any numbers for *a*, *b* and *c*, predict which algebraic expression will result in the greatest answer.

Which expression will result in the smallest answer?

Which expressions will result in the same answer?

Now substitute positive whole numbers for the letters *a*, *b* and *c* and test your predictions.

What generalisations can you make?

$a + (b - c)$     $a + b + c$

$(a - b) + c$     $a - (b + c)$

$a - b - c$     $(a + b) - c$

## Think about ...

Remember, you need to make predictions before you substitute positive whole numbers for the letters. Can you explain how you arrived at your predictions?

Be sure to substitute different sets of three positive whole numbers to test your predictions.

## What if?

Which of these expressions will result in the greatest answer?

Which of these expressions will result in the smallest answer?

Which expressions will result in the same answer?

$a \times (b - c)$     $(a \times b) + c$     $(a \times b) - c$

$(a - b) \times c$     $a + (b \times c)$     $(a + b) \times c$

When you've finished, turn to page 80.

What generalisations can you make?

## Challenge

This is a magic square.

The sum of each column, row and diagonal is the same – this is the magic number.

What is the magic number for this magic square?

| 8 | 16 | 9 |
|---|----|---|
| 12 | 11 | 10 |
| 13 | 6 | 14 |

Investigate making magic squares using different positive whole number values for $a$, $b$ and $c$.

What is the magic number for each square you make?

| $a - c$ | $a + b + c$ | $a - b$ |
|---------|-------------|---------|
| $a - b + c$ | $a$ | $a + b - c$ |
| $a + b$ | $a - b - c$ | $a + c$ |

## Think about ...

When creating your own magic squares, think about which square you should start with and the order in which you work out what numbers go in the other squares.

For the 'What if?', remember that each column, row and diagonal of three squares must total 36.

## What if?

Make a magic square where the magic number is 36.

When you've finished, turn to page 80.

# Metric and imperial measures

## Challenge

Measure the length, mass and/or capacity of the objects collected, using metric measures.

Then use the table to convert the metric measures to imperial measures.

### Metric to imperial conversion table

| Multiply | by | to obtain |
|---|---|---|
| centimetres | 0·39 | inches |
| metres | 3·28 | feet |
| metres | 1·09 | yards |
| kilometres | 0·62 | miles |
| grams | 0·04 | ounces |
| kilograms | 2·2 | pounds |
| millilitres | 0·04 | fluid ounces |
| litres | 1·75 | pints |
| litres | 0·22 | gallons |

**You will need:**
- various classroom objects to measure
- measuring equipment (metric and imperial)

## Think about ...

Be sure to measure each object as accurately as possible.

Think carefully about how to use the conversion tables when converting mixed units such as 2 m 35 cm or $2\frac{1}{2}$ kg.

## What if?

### Imperial to metric conversion table

| Multiply | by | to obtain |
|---|---|---|
| inches | 2·54 | centimetres |
| feet | 0·3 | metres |
| yards | 0·91 | metres |
| miles | 1·61 | kilometres |
| ounces | 28·35 | grams |
| pounds | 0·45 | kilograms |
| fluid ounces | 28·41 | millilitres |
| pints | 0·57 | litres |
| gallons | 4·55 | litres |

Now collect some different objects to measure.

This time, measure the length, mass and/or capacity of the objects using imperial measures.

Then use this table to convert the imperial measures to metric measures.

When you've finished, turn to page 80.

# Time differences

## Challenge

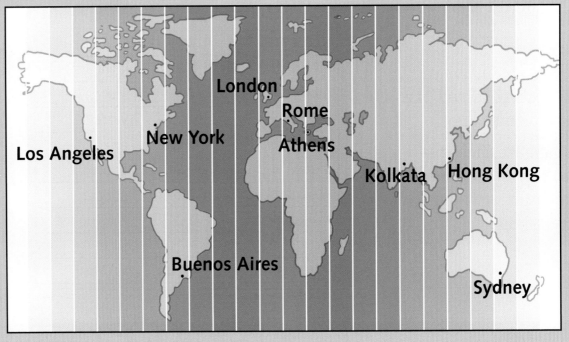

Investigate the time difference between London and the other cities on the map.

## Think about ...

Would your results be the same if you repeated this challenge in six months' time? Why?

Think about how to display your results for the 'What if?'.

## What if?

Investigate what time it would be in each of the other eight cities if it were:

| | |
|---|---|
| 12:00 in Los Angeles | 22:00 in Athens |
| 09:30 in New York | 23:00 in Kolkata |
| 06:30 in Buenos Aires | 14:00 in Hong Kong |
| 05:00 in London | 17:30 in Sydney |
| 16:00 in Rome | |

When you've finished, turn to page 80.

# VAT

## Challenge

VAT stands for Value Added Tax.

It is a tax added to the value of an item that is paid by the consumer when they buy the item.

All countries in Europe add VAT to the price of items, but at different rates.

The table below shows the different VAT rates for some countries in the European Union (EU) that use the Euro (€) as the local currency.

| Country | VAT rate |
|---|---|
| Luxembourg | 17% |
| Germany | 19% |
| France | 20% |
| Spain | 21% |
| Italy | 22% |
| Ireland | 23% |
| Finland | 24% |

This is how to calculate the price of an item including VAT:

(price of item before VAT × percentage rate of VAT) + price of item.

For example, to work out the price of these sunglasses in Luxembourg, including VAT:

(€24 × 0·17) + €24

= €4.08 + €24

= €28.08

Use the table to work out the price of the same pair of sunglasses in each of the other EU countries in the table.

Show all your calculations and working out.

## Think about ...

'exc' stands for 'excluding', which means the price before VAT is added.

Use known percentages, such as 1% and 10%, to help you work out unknown percentages.

## What if?

Without having to work out the exact price, which is the cheapest EU country in the table to buy the scooter?

Which is the most expensive country?

Explain why.

What is the difference in the price of the scooter in these two countries?

Show all your calculations and working out.

When you've finished, turn to page 80.

## Challenge

A farmer calculated the perimeter and area of all the fields on his farm.

Use this information to work out the dimensions of each field.

**You will need:**
- squared paper
- ruler

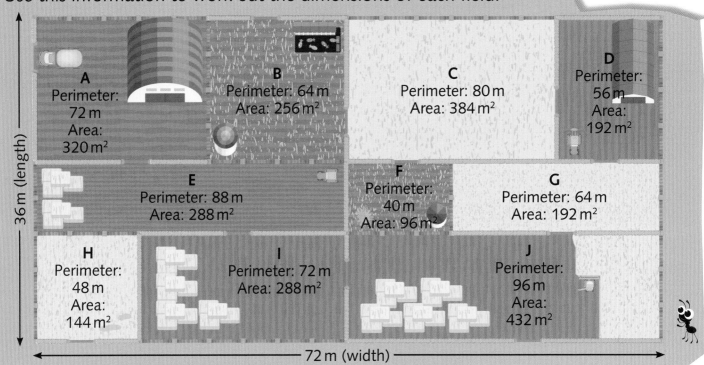

36 m (length)

**A**
Perimeter: 72 m
Area: 320 m²

**B**
Perimeter: 64 m
Area: 256 m²

**C**
Perimeter: 80 m
Area: 384 m²

**D**
Perimeter: 56 m
Area: 192 m²

**E**
Perimeter: 88 m
Area: 288 m²

**F**
Perimeter: 40 m
Area: 96 m²

**G**
Perimeter: 64 m
Area: 192 m²

**H**
Perimeter: 48 m
Area: 144 m²

**I**
Perimeter: 72 m
Area: 288 m²

**J**
Perimeter: 96 m
Area: 432 m²

72 m (width)

## Think about ...

Fields B and H are square fields.

The combined widths of fields A and B are the same as the combined widths of fields C and D.

The combined widths of fields A and B are the same width as field E, and the same width as the combined widths of fields H and I.

## What if?

Given the total area of the farm and the same number of fields, what other sizes could the fields be?

Use squared paper to show the dimensions of each field on the farm.

When you've finished, turn to page 80.

# Measuring temperature

## Challenge

Temperature is either measured in degrees Celsius (°C) or degrees Fahrenheit (°F).

> **To convert Celsius to Fahrenheit**
> Multiply by 9, then divide by 5, then add 32.

> **To convert Fahrenheit to Celsius**
> Subtract 32, then multiply by 5, then divide by 9.

Look for the temperature forecast in the weather section of a newspaper.

**You will need:**
- weather section from a newspaper

| 7 DAY FORECAST | | |
|---|---|---|
| PARIS | ☀ | 23°C |
| LONDON | ☁ | 12°C |
| DUBLIN | ☁ | 10°C |
| BERLIN | ⛅ | 18°C |
| OSLO | ☁ | 2°C |
| ROME | ☀ | 24°C |
| STOCKHOLM | ☁ | 5°C |
| LISBON | ☀ | 22°C |

Convert the temperatures in the newspaper from Celsius to Fahrenheit or from Fahrenheit to Celsius, using the temperature conversions on the left.

## Think about ...

Check carefully to see whether the temperatures in the newspaper are given in Celsius or Fahrenheit.

From the newspaper, choose the temperature forecast for around 10 different towns or cities.

## What if?

Copy and complete the table to show equivalent temperatures in degrees Celsius (°C) and degrees Fahrenheit (°F).

| Description | °C | °F |
|---|---|---|
| hot oven | 220 | |
| moderate oven | | 356 |
| water boils | 100 | |
| hot bath | | 104 |
| body temperature | 37 | |
| hot day | | 86 |
| room temperature | 21 | |
| cool day | | 50 |
| water freezes | 0 | |

When you've finished, turn to page 80.

25

## Challenge

Draw, or trace around, a regular hexagon.

Starting from one of the hexagon's vertices, draw the diagonals.

Draw all the diagonals in the hexagon.

What is the total number of diagonals in a hexagon?

Draw a square and a regular pentagon, heptagon and octagon, and investigate the total number of diagonals in each polygon.

**You will need:**
- set of regular 2-D shapes
- ruler
- coloured pencils

## Think about ...

Draw your polygons and diagonals as accurately as you can.

When colouring one of your polygons for the 'What if?', think about whether your pattern will show vertical, horizontal or diagonal symmetry.

## What if?

If $n$ represents the number of sides of a polygon, investigate this formula for calculating the number of diagonals:

$$\frac{(n-3) \times n}{2}$$

How do your results, using this formula, compare with your results from the 'Challenge' above?

Use the formula to find out the number of diagonals in these polygons:

         (octagon-like shape)

nonagon        decagon        hendecagon        dodecagon

Look at one of the polygons that you have drawn, including all the diagonals.

Colour the regions to make a symmetrical pattern.

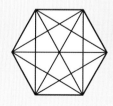

When you've finished, turn to page 80.

# Polygon angles

## Challenge

Draw, or trace around, a regular pentagon.

Choose any vertex and connect it to all the other vertices.

Count the number of triangles.

Multiply the number of triangles by 180° (the number of degrees in a triangle).

Investigate this method for calculating the sum of all the interior angles in other regular polygons.

**You will need:**
- set of regular 2-D shapes
- ruler

## Think about ...

Make sure that you find the sum of interior angles and the size of each angle in a square and a regular pentagon, hexagon, heptagon and octagon. Can you calculate the sum of the interior angles and the size of each angle of other polygons?

An interior angle is an angle inside a shape.

— interior angle

exterior angle

## What if?

If $n$ represents the number of sides of a polygon, investigate this formula for calculating the sum of all the interior angles: $(n - 2) \times 180$

How do your results, using this formula, compare with your results from the 'Challenge' above?

To work out the size of each angle in a regular polygon, you use this formula. Use the formula to calculate the size of each angle in regular polygons.

$$\frac{(n - 2) \times 180}{n}$$

When you've finished, turn to page 80.

## Challenge

Use either a four quadrant coordinates grid with vertical and horizontal axes marked to at least ± 6, or use squared paper to draw and label a four quadrant coordinates grid.

Draw a polygon so that it has at least one vertex in each of the four quadrants of the grid.

Write down the coordinates of your shape.

Reverse the signs of the coordinates.

Now draw a shape using these coordinates.

Investigate doing this for other polygons.

**You will need:**
- four quadrant coordinates grids or squared paper
- ruler

(2, 5), (−1, 5), (−3, 3),
(−3, 0), (−1, −2), (2, −2),
(4, 0), (4, 3), (−2, −5),
(1, −5), (3, −3), (3, 0), (1,

## Think about ...

Make sure that you carefully check the coordinates of the vertices for your polygons.

Can you predict where your translated shape will appear on the grid?

## What if?

Using only the digits 2, 3, 5 and 6, make different coordinates, for example: (−3, 5), (−2, −3), (2, 3), (6, −5).

Using these coordinates, what shapes can you make?

When you've finished, turn to page 80.

## Challenge

Use either a four quadrant coordinates grid with vertical and horizontal axes marked to at least ± 6, or use squared paper to draw and label a four quadrant coordinates grid.

Draw a polygon in the first quadrant.

Label the vertices A, B, C, D … and write down the coordinates for each vertex.

Draw the reflection of your design in the y-axis and then reflect both shapes in the x-axis.

Write the coordinates for the vertices of each of the three reflected shapes.

A (2, 5) B (5, 4), C (5, 2)

**You will need:**
- four quadrant coordinates grids or squared paper
- ruler
- coloured pencils

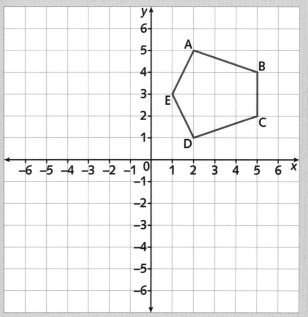

## Think about ...

Don't draw a quadrilateral as your polygon. Draw a polygon with at least five sides and vertices.

Draw the first quadrant polygon in an interesting orientation. Your polygon doesn't have to be regular.

When colouring your design for the 'What if?', think about whether your pattern will show vertical, horizontal or diagonal symmetry.

## What if?

Look at your completed design. Colour your design to make a symmetrical pattern.

When you've finished, turn to page 80.

## Challenge

The table on the right shows the results of a survey conducted by a local travel company to find out the type of holiday most people prefer to go on.

Using the information presented in the table, and the circle divided into tenths, draw a pie chart to show the results of the survey.

Make statements comparing the different types of holiday that people prefer to go on.

Which did you refer to most when making your statements: the table or your pie chart?

Explain why.

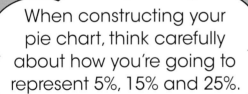

**You will need:**
- circle divided into tenths (faint division lines if possible)
- coloured pencils
- squared paper
- ruler

| Type of holiday | Percentage |
|---|---|
| Arts and culture | 10% |
| Activity and adventure | 25% |
| Cruise | 10% |
| Beach | 20% |
| Festivals and events | 5% |
| Safari and wildlife | 15% |
| Sports | 10% |
| Other | 5% |

## Think about ...

When constructing your pie chart, think carefully about how you're going to represent 5%, 15% and 25%.

Remember to include all the necessary features on your pie chart and bar chart so that they are easy to read and interpret.

## What if?

Use the information presented in the table to draw a bar chart on the squared paper showing the results of the survey.

Compare your bar chart with the table and your pie chart. Which of these three types of data presentation do you find easiest to read and interpret?

Explain why.

When you've finished, turn to page 80.

## Challenge

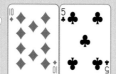  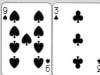

**You will need:**
- pack of playing cards with K, Q, J and Joker removed

The **average** is the value that is most typical of a set of data.

When we talk about 'the average', we are usually referring to the **mean**.

Shuffle a pack of playing cards (making sure that the K, Q, J and Joker have been removed) and place the cards face down in a pile on the table.

Take the top two cards, write down the numbers and work out the total.

Repeat 20 times until all 40 cards have been used.

Calculate the mean of the 20 totals.

We can use two other types of average to describe a set of data. They are called the **mode** and the **median**.

Calculate the mode and median of the 20 totals.

6, 3 (9)

8, 2 (10)

4, 4 (8)

5, 1 (6)

Consider an Ace as the number 1.

## Think about ...

The **mean** is the sum of all the values divided by the number of values.

The **mode** is the value that occurs most often. You can have more than one mode.

The **median** is the middle value when all the values are arranged in order. If there is an odd number of results, the median is the middle number. If there is an even number of results, the median will be the mean of the two middle numbers.

## What if?

What if you find the difference between each pair of numbers?

6, 3 (3)

8, 2 (6)

4, 4 (0)

5, 1 (4)

What if you find the product of each pair of numbers?

6, 3 (18)

8, 2 (16)

4, 4 (16)

5, 1 (5)

When you've finished, turn to page 80.

## Challenge

Ms Moore has these four number cards.
She gives one card to each pupil.

| 483 571 | 492 781 |
|---------|---------|
| 493 571 | 493 781 |

My number is 493 000 rounded to the nearest thousand.

My number card is 10 000 more than one of the other number cards.

The number on my card is between 493 600 and 493 800.

In my number, the value of the 8 is 80 000.

Which card does each child have?

Explain your reasoning.

## Think about ...

Reread the clues in a different order to make sure that you have matched each pupil with the correct card.

For the 'What if?', think about clues relating to place value, comparing and ordering numbers, and rounding numbers.

## What if?

Think of four different 5-digit, 6-digit or 7-digit numbers.

Write a set of clues for each number.

Each set of clues must lead to just one number.

Show your clues (but not the numbers) to a friend and ask them to work out what each of your four numbers are.

When you've finished, turn to page 80.

## Challenge

David, Eve, Johannes and Sofia each worked out the answers to these four calculations:

$$12 - 5 = \qquad 12 + 5 =$$
$$-12 - 5 = \qquad -12 + 5 =$$

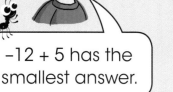
−12 − 5 and 12 + 5 both have the same answer.

−12 + 5 has the smallest answer.

The answer of each calculation is either 7 or 17.

Two of the answers are less than zero.

Do you agree with each pupil's statement? Explain your reasoning.

## Think about ...

In which direction on the number line do you move when you add a number? What about when you subtract a number?

Use a number line to help you work out the answers and explain your reasoning.

−20 −18 −16 −14 −12 −10 −8 −6 −4 −2 0 2 4 6 8 10 12 14 16 18 20

## What if?

Work out the answers to these calculations.

Explain how you worked out each answer.

$$5 - 8 - 3 =$$
$$-2 + 4 - 6 =$$
$$-1 - 5 + 8 =$$
$$3 - 7 + 10 =$$

When you've finished, turn to page 80.

## Challenge

Work out the answers to these calculations:

What patterns do you notice?

$11·1 + 1·11 =$

$22·2 + 2·22 =$

$33·3 + 3·33 =$

Now find the difference between consecutive answers.

What do you notice about these answers?

Can you predict what the answers will be for these calculations?

$111·1 + 1·111 =$

$222·2 + 2·222 =$

$333·3 + 3·333 =$

What about these calculations?

$111·11 + 11·111 =$

$222·22 + 22·222 =$

$333·33 + 33·333 =$

## Think about ...

For each set of calculations, write at least two more calculations to continue the pattern.

## What if?

What if you work out the answers to these calculations and then find the difference between consecutive answers?

$11·1 − 1·11 =$

$22·2 − 2·22 =$

$33·3 − 3·33 =$

$111·1 − 1·111 =$

$222·2 − 2·222 =$

$333·3 − 3·333 =$

$111·11 − 11·111 =$

$222·22 − 22·222 =$

$333·33 − 33·333 =$

What patterns do you notice?

When you've finished, turn to page 80.

## Challenge

Sofia uses this method to check whether a number to 100 is a prime number.

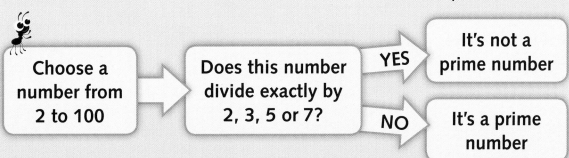

**Choose a number from 2 to 100** → **Does this number divide exactly by 2, 3, 5 or 7?** — YES → **It's not a prime number**

— NO → **It's a prime number**

Does Sofia's method work?

Explain why.

## Think about ...

Make sure that you choose a sufficient selection of numbers to be able to justify your decisions.

Include examples along with your explanations.

## What if?

The product of the lowest common multiple (LCM) and the greatest common factor (GCF) of any two numbers is always equal to the product of those two numbers.

Do you agree with Johannes' statement?

Explain why.

When you've finished, turn to page 80.

## Challenge

Without working out the answers, match each problem with its answer.

| | |
|---|---|
| 174 × 83 = | 14 242 |
| 30 831 − 16 587 = | $98\frac{2}{3}$ |
| 2368 ÷ 24 = | 14 400 |
| 6317 + 7925 = | 14 442 |
| $12^2$ × 100 = | $182\frac{5}{9}$ |
| 1643 ÷ 9 = | 14 244 |

Explain what you did to determine the correct answer.

## Think about ...

Think carefully about the different strategies to use when matching the problem with its answer. Write about these strategies in your explanations.

## What if?

Sofia, Eve, Johannes and David each worked out the answer to this calculation:

**872 ÷ 32 =**

Here are their answers.

**Sofia**
$872 ÷ 32 = 27\frac{1}{4}$

**Eve**
$872 ÷ 32 = 27 \text{ r } 4$

**Johannes**
$872 ÷ 32 = 27\frac{8}{32}$

**David**
$872 ÷ 32 = 27·25$

Ms Moore says: Three of you have worked out the correct answer.

Who hasn't worked out the correct answer? What should the answer be?

How can the other three answers all be correct?

When you've finished, turn to page 80.

## Challenge

For each calculation, which is the correct answer, A, B, C or D?

Explain why.

**1.** 7 + 4 × 5
A. 55
B. 16
C. 27
D. 54

**2.** 160 – 5 × 6
A. 130
B. 90
C. 360
D. 930

**3.** (92 – 10) × 5
A. 87
B. 42
C. 77
D. 410

**4.** 9 × (16 – 7)
A. 72
B. 127
C. 137
D. 81

**5.** (12 – 6) × (4 – 1)
A. 24
B. 18
C. 13
D. 20

**6.** 24 ÷ (12 – 4)
A. 8
B. 4
C. 3
D. –2

**7.** 60 – 30 ÷ 6
A. 55
B. 36
C. 50
D. 5

**8.** 18 – 3 × 6
A. 9
B. 90
C. 0
D. 19

## Think about ...

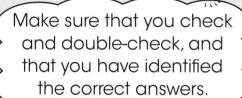

Make sure that you check and double-check, and that you have identified the correct answers.

For the 'What if?', what advice would you give Sofia to help her ensure that she doesn't make the same mistakes again?

## What if?

Sofia answered these questions.

Draw a ring around the correct answer.

**1.** 20 + 4 × 5 ÷ 10
A. 12 ⟵(ringed)
B. 28
C. 21
D. 22

**2.** (9 + 2) × 6
A. 63
B. 66 ⟵(ringed)
C. 21
D. 22

**3.** 36 ÷ (12 – 3)
A. 19
B. 0 ⟵(ringed)
C. 4
D. 6

**4.** 10 + 6 × 3 – 5
A. 53
B. 43
C. 23 ⟵(ringed)
D. 13

Mark Sofia's work.

For each of Sofia's incorrect answers, can you explain the mistakes she made?

When you've finished, turn to page 80.

# Order the fractions

## Challenge

Without working out the answers, predict which of these four calculations will result in the greatest answer.

$$\frac{2}{3} + \frac{3}{5}$$ $$\frac{3}{4} - \frac{1}{3}$$ $$\frac{4}{5} \times \frac{3}{4}$$ $$\frac{5}{6} \div 5$$

Which calculation will give the smallest answer?

Justify your predictions.

What about these four calculations? Predict which will give the greatest and smallest answers. Why do you think those calculations will give the greatest and smallest answers?

$$\frac{3}{4} + \frac{1}{6}$$ $$\frac{5}{6} - \frac{3}{4}$$ $$\frac{1}{3} \times \frac{3}{8}$$ $$\frac{2}{5} \div 4$$

## Think about ...

What mental images can you create to help you determine which calculations will give the greatest and smallest answers?

Think about what happens to the size of a fraction when you add, subtract or multiply it by another fraction, or divide it by a whole number. Does the fraction become larger or smaller?

## What if?

Ms Moore taught her class how algebra can be used to help remember how to add, subtract, multiply and divide fractions.

| Adding fractions | Subtracting fractions | Multiplying fractions | Dividing fractions by a whole number |
|---|---|---|---|
| $\frac{a}{b} + \frac{c}{d} = \frac{ad + bc}{bd}$ | $\frac{a}{b} - \frac{c}{d} = \frac{ad - bc}{bd}$ | $\frac{a}{b} \times \frac{c}{d} = \frac{ac}{bd}$ | $\frac{a}{b} \div c = \frac{a}{bc}$ |

Use Ms Moore's algebraic formulae to work out the answer to each of the calculations above to check your predictions.

When you've finished, turn to page 80.

## Challenge

Johannes, David, Sofia and Eve were all given the same calculation to work out. Here is how they each calculated the correct answer.

Which of these methods would you choose to use to solve a similar calculation? Why?

Which of the methods above would you never use? Why?

Would you use a different method? If so, what is it?

**3·48 × 7**

**Johannes**

| × | 3 | 0·4 | 0·08 |
|---|---|-----|------|
| 7 | 21 | 2·8 | 0·56 | = 24·36

**David**

```
    348
×   3 5 7
  2 4 3 6
```
$2436 \div 100 = 24.36$

**Sofia**

```
    3·48
×      7
    0·56   (7 × 0·08)
    2·80   (7 × 0·4)
+  21·00   (7 × 3)
   24·36
```

**Eve**

```
    348
×      7
     56   (7 × 8)
    280   (7 × 40)
+  2100   (7 × 300)
   2436
```
$2436 \div 100 = 24.36$

## Think about ...

Which method gives you the answer the quickest? Which method is the most consistent for getting the correct answer?

Your preferred method might not be exactly the same as one of the methods above. How is it different?

## What if?

Which of these methods would you choose to use to solve the division calculation? Why?

**38·24 ÷ 4**

Would you use a different method? If so, what is it?

**Sofia**

```
      9·56
  4)38·24
  -36·00
    2·24
  -  2·00
    0·24
  -  0·24
       0
```

**David**

```
      9· 5 6
  4)3 8 ·²2²4
```

**Eve**

```
      9 5 6
  4)3 8²2²4
```
$956 \div 100 = 9.56$

When you've finished, turn to page 80.

## Challenge

Eve sorted a set of fractions, decimals and percentages cards.

Has she paired equivalent fractions, decimals and percentages?

Explain your reasoning.

For each pair of cards, write the missing equivalent fraction, decimal or percentage.

| 25% | 0·2 |

| 40% | $\frac{1}{25}$ |

| $\frac{5}{10}$ | 5% |

| 54% | 0·54 |

| 0·125 | $\frac{1}{8}$ |

| $\frac{1}{20}$ | 0·5 |

| $\frac{3}{4}$ | 60% |

| 0·75 | $\frac{3}{5}$ |

| 0·25 | 20% |

| 0·4 | 4% |

## Think about ...

Use equivalent fractions, decimals and percentages that you know to help you find equivalent fractions, decimals and percentages that you don't know.

Think about how equivalent fractions can help you find equivalent decimals and percentages.

## What if?

Look at all the fractions, decimals and percentages above.

Order all the fractions, from smallest to greatest.

Round decimals with 2 decimal places to the nearest tenth.

Round decimals with 3 decimal places to the nearest hundredth and tenth.

Arrange the percentages into two groups: those less than 50% and those 50% or more.

When you've finished, turn to page 80.

## Challenge

I can easily work out 1%, 10%, 25% and 50% of a number or quantity.

Explain why David finds it easy to work out these percentages.

Use examples to help illustrate your explanation.

David also says:

In fact, I can use 1%, 10%, 25% and 50% to help me find any percentage of a number.

Explain David's method for working out any percentage of a number.

## Think about ...

Use different whole numbers and quantities to illustrate your explanations.

Think about the relationship between fractions, decimals and percentages.

## What if?

Ms Moore asks:

David, how would you work out 12·5% of a number?

When you've finished, turn to page 80.

How might David work this out?

41

# Describe the towers

## Challenge

Eve, David, Johannes, Sofia and Ms Moore have each built two towers of interlocking cubes.

Match each pupil to their two towers.

The ratio of blue to red in my two towers is 3 : 4 and 3 : 7.

The ratio of red to blue in one of my towers is 1 : 3. The ratio of blue to red in my other tower is 2 : 3.

The ratio of red to blue in one of my towers is 1 : 2. The ratio of red to blue in my other tower is 3 : 5.

The ratio of red to blue in my two towers is 2 : 5 and 1 : 5.

Ms Moore built the remaining two towers. Which two towers did she build? What is the ratio of red cubes to blue cubes in Ms Moore's two towers?

## Think about ...

**Ratio** tells us how much we have of one amount compared to another amount.

**Proportion** tells us how much we have of something compared to the whole amount.

## What if?

Sofia says:

Describe the proportion of blue cubes to red cubes for each of the other towers.

In one of my towers, $\frac{2}{5}$ of the cubes are blue and $\frac{3}{5}$ of the cubes are red. In my other tower, $\frac{3}{4}$ of the cubes are blue and $\frac{1}{4}$ are red.

When you've finished, turn to page 80.

42

## Challenge

**You will need:**
- squared paper
- ruler
- coloured pencils (optional)

If $a =$  and $b =$  then:  $= a + b$

Write an expression for each of these shapes.

Draw two shapes that can be represented by each of these expressions.

**$2a + b$**    **$2a + 2b$**    **$1\frac{1}{2}a + b$**

## Think about ...

Draw your shapes as accurately as possible.

Think about how to represent the semicircle: $+ b$ or $- b$.

## What if?

This diagram shows $a - b$:

Write an expression for each of these shapes.

Draw two shapes that can be represented by each of these expressions.

When you've finished, turn to page 80.

**$3a - b$**    **$3a - 2b$**    **$1\frac{1}{2}a - b$**

# What are the numbers?

## Challenge

I've thought of three different positive whole numbers, $a$, $b$ and $c$, which are all less than 10. When I work out $a + b$ the answer is 12, when I work out $b + c$ the answer is 7, and when I work out $a + c$ the answer is 13.

What are Sofia's three numbers?

Explain how you worked out Sofia's three numbers.

## Think about ...

Is it possible that Sofia or David could have chosen a different set of three numbers?

When writing your own problems for the second 'What if?' task, you might decide to use bigger numbers, for example numbers less than 20.

## What if?

I have thought of three positive whole numbers, $a$, $b$ and $c$, all less than 10. When I work out $a - b$ the answer is 3, when I work out $a - c$ the answer is 6, and when I work out $c - b$ the answer is –3.

What are David's three numbers?

Explain how you worked out David's three numbers.

Now make up two problems like Sofia's and David's for a friend to solve.

When you've finished, turn to page 80.

## Challenge

I've got ½ litre of apple juice.

I've got ½ pint of apple juice.

I've got 700 grams of sweets.

I've got 1 pound of sweets.

I've got 15 inches of liquorice.

I've got 30 centimetres of liquorice.

For each pair of pupils, who has more?

Explain why.

## Think about ...

Think about how to convert metric and imperial measurements of length, mass and volume.

You will need to round measurements to a suitable level of accuracy.

## What if?

Altogether, how much apple juice do Sofia and David have?

What is the total mass of sweets that Johannes and Eve have?

What is the combined length of liquorice that Eve and David have?

Which units of measurement are you going to use? Why?

Explain how you worked out each answer.

When you've finished, turn to page 80.

## Challenge

We don't use decimals to describe time. However, we do say things like:

> I'll see you in two and a half hours time.

> The cake will take one and a quarter hours to cook.

> It's three quarters of an hour until lunch.

How would you express $2\frac{1}{2}$ hours, $1\frac{1}{4}$ hours and $\frac{3}{4}$ of an hour using decimals?

Explain your answers.

## Think about ...

> Think carefully about fraction and decimal equivalences.

> Use known expressions that you can recall easily to help you work out unknown expressions.

## What if?

What would each of these time durations be in hours and minutes?

| 2·1 hours | 5·3 hours | 1·8 hours | 2·9 hours | 3·6 hours |

Explain your answers.

How would you express each of these time durations as a decimal?

| 3 hours and 12 minutes | 1 hour and 42 minutes |

| 4 hours and 24 minutes |

When you've finished, turn to page 80.

Explain your answers.

## Challenge

| | | |
|---|---|---|
| Total earned in four hours if you were paid £8.43 an hour. | $\frac{5}{8}$ of £54 | Your share of £202.44 shared between 6 people. |
| The total of £9.25, £12.87 and £11.64. | The change from £50 after spending £16.23. | 15% of £225 |

Which amount would you rather have?

Explain your thinking.

## Think about ...

Show all your working out.

Make sure that you check your work. Think about how you are going to do this.

## What if?

Ms Moore is buying a car for £8730. She is going to pay this amount in 12 equal monthly instalments.

She works out how much she has to pay each month.

$$12 \overline{\smash{)}8\,7\,{}^3 3\,{}^9 0} = 7\,2\,7\,\text{r}\,6$$

So that means I have to pay £727.60 each month.

Is Ms Moore correct?

Explain why.

When you've finished, turn to page 80.

47

## Challenge

Eve, Sofia and David each worked out the correct area of Shape A. On the right are the calculations that the pupils did to work out the shape's area.

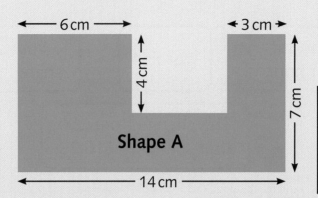

**Shape A**

**You will need:**
• squared paper
• ruler

Eve
$(6 \times 7) + (5 \times 3) + (3 \times 7)$
$= 42 + 15 + 21$
$= 78 \, cm^2$

Sofia
$(6 \times 4) + (3 \times 4) + (14 \times 3)$
$= 24 + 12 + 42$
$= 78 \, cm^2$

David
$(14 \times 7) - (5 \times 4)$
$= 98 - 20$
$= 78 \, cm^2$

Explain how each pupil worked out the area.

## Think about ...

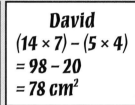

If necessary, use a sketch to help describe how each pupil worked out the area and perimeter.

For the second 'What if?' task, draw and label your shapes as accurately as possible.

## What if?

The three pupils also calculated the perimeter of Shape A. However, they each got a different answer.

Who worked out the correct perimeter?

How did the other two pupils work out the perimeter?

Eve
$6 + 7 + 6 + 7 + 5 + 3 + 5 + 3$
$+ 3 + 7 + 3 + 7 = 62 \, cm$

David
$6 + 3 + 14 + 4$
$+ 7 = 34 \, cm$

Sofia
$6 + 4 + 5 + 4 + 3 + 7 + 14 + 7 = 50 \, cm$

The area of Shape A is 78 cm². Draw a shape that also has an area of 78 cm², but where the perimeter is different from Shape A.

Now draw a shape that has the same perimeter as Shape A, but a different area.

When you've finished, turn to page 80.

# Formula for what?

## Challenge

Ms Moore has been teaching her Year 6 class the formulae for calculating the area, perimeter and volume of different shapes.

She wrote these formulae on the whiteboard.

Can you identify what each formula is used to calculate?

Explain how you know what each formula is for.

**You will need:**
- squared paper
- ruler

$$lwh \qquad \frac{1}{2}bh$$

$$bh \qquad 2(l+w)$$

$$4l \qquad lw$$

## Think about ...

*l* stands for **length**, *w* stands for **width**, *b* stands for **base**, and *h* stands for **height**.

Remember that in algebra, *bh* is the same as *b* × *h*, and 4*l* is the same as 4 × *l*.

## What if?

Use each of the formulae on the whiteboard above to calculate the area, perimeter and volume of different shapes.

Draw each shape and label the dimensions of the shape.

Show your working out.

When you've finished, turn to page 80.

## Challenge

A scalene triangle has no equal sides.

The angles inside a quadrilateral always total 360°.

Are these statements true or false?

Every quadrilateral is a parallelogram.

The angles inside a triangle always add up to 180°.

An isosceles triangle has three equal sides.

A triangle can have two obtuse angles.

Every rhombus is a parallelogram.

Every square is a rhombus.

In a polygon, the number of its sides is always the same as the number of its angles.

Every square is a rectangle.

Every parallelogram is a rectangle.

The more sides a polygon has, the greater the size of each interior angle.

Every rectangle is a parallelogram.

Every trapezium is a rhombus.

All 2-D shapes are polygons.

In a regular shape, all sides are equal and all angles are equal.

If your answer is false, explain why it is false.

Every hexagon has six equal sides and six equal angles.

**You will need:**
- squared paper
- ruler

## Think about …

You may want to draw an example when explaining why a statement is false.

Use your decisions about the statements in the 'Challenge' to help you complete the 'What if?'.

## What if?

Redraw this flowchart.

Write the name of each quadrilateral and include a diagram to represent each quadrilateral.

quadrilateral

two sets of parallel sides

one pair of parallel sides

no sides are parallel

all sides are equal

all angles are equal

all sides and angles are equal

When you've finished, turn to page 80.

# Forgotten angles

## Challenge

Johannes calculated the size of the missing angles in each of these shapes. However, he forgot to write the letter for each angle beside its correct size in the table.

Work out which letter, a to k, belongs to each angle.

Explain how you know.

**You will need:**
- ruler
- protractor (optional)

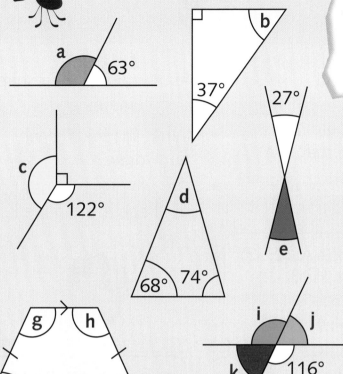

| Letter | Size of angle |
|--------|---------------|
|        | 148°          |
|        | 115°          |
|        | 27°           |
|        | 117°          |
|        | 64°           |
|        | 53°           |
|        | 115°          |
|        | 116°          |
|        | 38°           |
|        | 64°           |
|        | 65°           |

## Think about ...

You need to **calculate** the size of the missing angles, not **measure** them.

For the 'What if?', draw your diagram as accurately as you can.

## What if?

Three angles meet around a point.

One of the angles is a right angle.

The other two angles are equal.

What size are the other two angles?

Draw a diagram to prove it.

---

Four angles meet on a straight line.

One angle is 66°.

The other three angles are equal.

What size are the other three angles?

Draw a diagram to prove it.

When you've finished, turn to page 80.

51

## Challenge

Sofia, Eve, Johannes and David each drew a different shape on a four quadrant coordinates grid and labelled their shape 'A'.

Then they each translated their shape and labelled the translated shape 'B'.

Without drawing their shapes on a coordinates grid:

- What shape did each pupil draw?
- Describe each translation of Shape A to Shape B.

**You will need:**
- four quadrant coordinates grids or squared paper
- ruler

Shape A: (2, –2) (2, 1) (3, –2)
Shape B: (4, 3) (4, 6) (5, 3)

Shape A: (–4, 3) (–4, 5) (–2, 5) (–2, 3)
Shape B: (1,3) (1, 5) (3, 5) (3, 3)

Shape A: (–3, 1) (–3, 2) (1, 2) (1, 1)
Shape B: (–6, –5) (–6, –4) (–2, –4) (–2, –5)

Shape A: (5, –3) (2, –3) (1, –5) (4, –5)
Shape B: (–1, –1) (–4, –1) (–5, –3) (–2, –3)

## Think about ...

For the 'Challenge', you are using mental imagery to work out what shape each pupil drew, and how each pupil translated their Shape A to Shape B.

Remember, for the 'What if?', use just one coordinates grid to plot all eight shapes.

## What if?

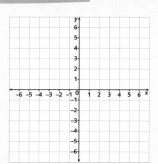

Use either a four quadrant coordinates grid with vertical and horizontal axes marked to ± 6, or use squared paper to draw and label a four quadrant coordinates grid.

Plot both shapes for each pupil on the one grid to check your answers. Label each pupil's two shapes: 'A' and 'B'.

When you've finished, turn to page 80.

## Challenge

Sofia, Eve, Johannes and David each drew a different shape on a four quadrant coordinates grid and labelled their shape 'A'.

Then they each reflected their shape in the x- or y-axis and labelled the reflected shape 'B'.

Without drawing their shapes on a coordinates grid:

- What shape did each pupil draw?

- What are the coordinates of the reflected shape ('B')?

**You will need:**

- four quadrant coordinates grids or squared paper
- ruler

Shape A: (3, 1) (3, 3) (5, 3) (5, 1)
I reflected Shape A in the y-axis.

Shape A: (−3, −4) (−5, −3) (−5, 0) (−3, −1)
I reflected Shape A in the y-axis.

Shape A: (1, −3) (0, −5) (3, −5) (2, −3)
I reflected Shape A in the x-axis.

Shape A: (−2, 4) (−3, 6) (−1, 6)
I reflected Shape A in the x-axis.

## Think about ...

For the 'Challenge', you are using mental imagery to work out what shape each pupil drew, and the coordinates of each pupil's Shape B.

Remember, for the 'What if?', use just one coordinates grid to plot all eight shapes.

## What if?

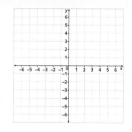

Use either a four quadrant coordinates grid with vertical and horizontal axes marked to ± 6, or use squared paper to draw and label a four quadrant coordinates grid.

Plot both shapes for each pupil on the one grid to check your answers. Label each pupil's two shapes: 'A' and 'B'.

When you've finished, turn to page 80.

## Challenge

What could each of these pie charts be showing?

What conclusions can you make from the data in each of these pie charts?

**Pie chart A**

**Pie chart B**

## Think about ...

The different slices or sections of a pie chart may be referred to as **sectors**.

For the 'Challenge', think of a different 'story' for each graph.

For the 'What if?', think about the same story.

In your descriptions and comparisons of the pie charts, include numbers or percentages.

## What if?

Each of the pie charts above consists of five sectors – each sector is a different colour.

Compare the same sectors in the two pie charts, that is the green sector in Pie chart A with the green sector in Pie chart B, the blue sector in Pie chart A with the blue sector in Pie chart B and so on.

What comparisons and conclusions can you make?

When you've finished, turn to page 80.

54

2 3 4 6 2 1

6 2 5 4 2 5

## Challenge

Ms Moore rolled a 1–6 dice 12 times and wrote the 12 numbers on the board.

She then asked the pupils in her class to each choose between five and 12 of the numbers and work out the mean.

I chose six numbers and the mean number is 4.

The mean of my seven numbers is 3.

I chose eight numbers. The mean is 3.

I chose ten numbers and the mean is 3·5.

What numbers did Eve, David, Sofia and Johannes choose?

Explain your thinking.

## Think about ...

Show all your working out.

Think carefully about your answer to the 'What if?' question.

## What if?

Ms Moore rolled the dice twice more and said:

The mean of all 14 dice rolls is 3·5.

What two numbers might Ms Moore have rolled?

Explain your thinking.

When you've finished, turn to page 80.

## Challenge

Look at this sequence of numbers:

# 1, 1, 2, 3, 5, 8, 13, 21, 34, 55, ...

Describe how the sequence is created.

What is the name given to this special number sequence?

What is 'special' about this number sequence?

Write the next 10 numbers in the sequence.

## Think about ...

What patterns do you notice? What is the rule for describing this sequence?

What makes this number sequence so special?

## What if?

Add together the first 5 numbers in the sequence. Write down the answer.

Then add the first 6 numbers and write down the answer.

Next, add the first 7 numbers and write down the answer.

Finally, add the first 8 numbers and write down the answer.

Look at the four answers you have just written down.

Compare these with the numbers of the sequence above.

What do you notice?

Can you predict what the sum of the first 9, 10, 11, ... numbers are?

When you've finished, turn to page 80.

## Challenge

Look at the ten numbers in the number sequence on page 56.

Choose four consecutive numbers in the sequence.

Find the products of the first and last numbers, and the second and third numbers.

Now work out the difference between the two products.

Choose four more consecutive numbers in the sequence and repeat the above.

What do you notice?

## Think about ...

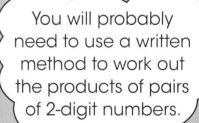

Remember, consecutive numbers are numbers that follow each other in order, without gaps. For example, 10, 11, 12 and 13 are consecutive counting numbers; whereas 2, 4, 6 and 8 are consecutive even numbers.

You will probably need to use a written method to work out the products of pairs of 2-digit numbers.

## What if?

Choose three consecutive numbers from the sequence.

Multiply the first and last numbers together, and square the second number.

Now work out the difference between the two products.

Choose three more consecutive numbers from the sequence and repeat the above.

What do you notice?

When you've finished, turn to page 80.

# Pascal's triangle

## Challenge

This triangular pattern of numbers was discovered in 1653 by a French mathematician named Blaise Pascal.

```
              1
           1     1
        1     2     1
        1     3     3     1
     1     4     6     4     1
  1     5     10    10    5     1
```

What is the pattern?

Write the next two rows of the pattern at the base of the triangle.

## Think about ...

You will need to write the first six rows as shown above. Carefully draw Pascal's triangle so that you can spot any patterns.

You could include a diagram along with your description, explaining what patterns you notice.

## What if?

Ms Moore says:

A 'power' tells us how many of the same number are multiplied together.
$2 \times 2$ is shortened to $2^2$, where 2 is the power. We say it as '2 to the power of 2' or '2 squared'.
$2 \times 2 \times 2$ is shortened to $2^3$, where 3 is the power. We say it as '2 to the power of 3'.

$$2^2 = 2 \times 2 = 4$$
$$2^3 = 2 \times 2 \times 2 = 8$$
$$2^4 = 2 \times 2 \times 2 \times 2 = 16$$

Investigate the link between Pascal's triangle and 2 and its powers.

Can you predict what the sum of rows 10, 11 and 12 will be?

When you've finished, turn to page 80.

# Patterns in Pascal's triangle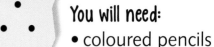

## Challenge

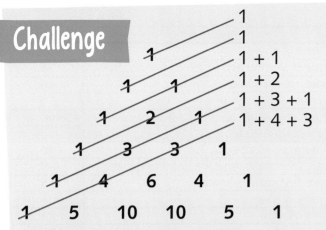

```
            1
            1
        1   1 + 1
      1   1 1 + 2
    1   2   1 1 + 3 + 1
                1 + 4 + 3
  1   3   3   1
 1   4   6   4   1
1   5   10  10  5   1
```

Investigate the sum of the diagonals in Pascal's triangle.

What patterns do you notice?

**You will need:**
• coloured pencils

Investigate the link between Pascal's triangle and triangular numbers.

What patterns do you notice?

What other patterns can you spot in Pascal's triangle?

## Think about ...

You could include diagrams along with your descriptions, explaining what patterns you notice.

## What if?

When you divide a number by 2, the remainder is 0 or 1.

Colour each number in Pascal's triangle according to its remainder.

What pattern do you notice?

When you divide a number by 3 the remainder is 0, 1 or 2.

Divide the numbers in Pascal's triangle by 3 and colour each one according to its remainder.

What pattern do you notice?

What about the patterns you get when you divide by other numbers?

Can you explain the pattern?

When you've finished, turn to page 80.

## Challenge

'If the world were 100 people' is a description of the world's population represented by 100 people.

We can see from the table that almost one fifth of the world's population don't have electricity.

We can also see that there are twice as many people on the planet that speak Chinese as speak Spanish.

What other statements can you make about the world's population, using the proportions given in the table?

| | People who: | Percentage |
|---|---|---|
| Gender | are male | 50 |
| Age | are under the age of 15 | 25 |
| | are aged 16 to 64 | 66 |
| | are over the age of 64 | 9 |
| Geography | are from Asia | 60 |
| | are from Africa | 16 |
| | are from Europe | 10 |
| | are from Latin America and the Caribbean | 9 |
| | are from North America | 5 |
| Religion | are Christian | 31 |
| | are Muslim | 23 |
| | are Hindu | 15 |
| | are of other faiths | 15 |
| | are of no faith or religion | 16 |
| First language | speak Chinese | 12 |
| | speak Spanish | 6 |
| | speak English | 5 |
| | speak Hindi | 4 |
| | speak other languages | 73 |
| Literacy | are unable to read and write | 14 |
| Education | have had a primary school education | 77 |
| | have had a secondary school education | 64 |
| | have studied at college or university | 7 |
| Dwellers | live in a city | 54 |
| | live in the country | 46 |
| Drinking water | have access to safe drinking water | 91 |
| Food | are undernourished | 11 |
| Electricity | do not have electricity | 18 |
| Technology | have a mobile phone | 65 |
| | are active internet users | 47 |

## Think about ...

Express your statements in different ways, such as using fractions rather than always using percentages. Also use terms such as 'more than', 'less than', 'around', 'about' and 'approximately'.

For the 'What if'?, use known percentages, such as 50% and 10%, to help you work out other percentages.

## What if?

There are approximately 8 billion (8 000 000 000) people in the world. This means that there are around 4 billion males in the world.

Look at the table above and work out the approximate number of people there are in the world for each of the other criteria.

When you've finished, turn to page 80.

# Who gets what?

## Challenge

This pie chart shows who gets the money when you buy an item of clothing produced in developing countries.

Investigate how much each group in the pie chart gets of the money you pay for an item of clothing.

If the average wage in developing countries is about £5 per week, how many items of your clothing would a factory worker have to make to earn this amount?

**You will need:**
- prices for different items of clothing

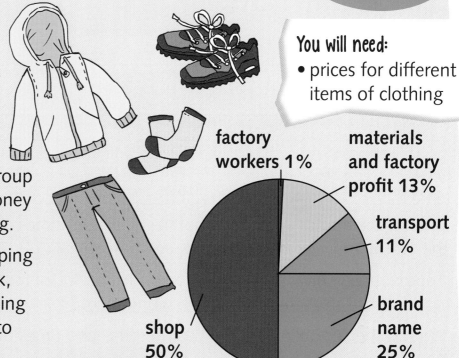

factory workers 1%

materials and factory profit 13%

transport 11%

brand name 25%

shop 50%

## Think about ...

If necessary, round the prices for your items of clothing to the nearest pound.

Choose at least three or four items of clothing, including shoes.

## What if?

A worker in a developing country who makes a pair of jeans that are sold for £37 in a shop in the UK is paid about 37p.

If you were paid this amount to make a pair of jeans, how many pairs would you have to make to pay for:

- a burger and chips?
- a ticket to the cinema?
- a computer game?

When you've finished, turn to page 80.

Think about other things you spend money on and how many pairs of jeans you would have to make in order to be able to pay for them.

# Running ratios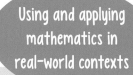

**Using and applying mathematics in real-world contexts**

## Challenge

**You will need:**
- stopwatch

| World record holders | | | |
|---|---|---|---|
| Male | | Female | |
| 100 m race | 400 m race | 100 m race | 400 m race |
| Usain Bolt 2009 9.58 seconds | Wayde van Niekerk 2016 43.03 seconds | Florence Griffith-Joyner 1988 10.49 seconds | Marita Koch 1985 47.60 seconds |

What is the approximate ratio between the two times of the 100 m and 400 m male world record holders?

Approximately how many times longer is the 400 m male world record than the 100 m male world record?

What is the approximate ratio between the two times of the 100 m and 400 m female world record holders?

Approximately how many times longer is the 400 m female world record than the 100 m female world record?

Now time yourself running 100 m and 400 m.

Calculate the approximate ratio between your two times.

How does your ratio compare to the ratios of the record holders?

## Think about ...

Remember, ratios compare two numbers or amounts and are used to show how much bigger or smaller one is than the other.

You will need to do some rounding before working out the ratios.

## What if?

Compare your ratio with other children in your class.

What conclusions can you draw?

When you've finished, turn to page 80.

# Everyday algebraic expressions

## Challenge

**Pineapples £4 each**

We use algebra every day to work out problems without even realising it.

For example:

If you want to buy three pineapples ($p$), you can calculate the total ($t$) amount using the algebraic equation: $t = 3p$

If you pay for the total ($t$) cost of three pineapples with a £20 note, you work out how much change ($c$) you would receive using the algebraic equation: $c = 20 - t$

How might you express each of these scenarios as an algebraic equation?

Elsa ($e$) is 3 years old. Daniel ($d$) is 5 years older than Elsa. How old is Daniel?

There are 52 children ($c$) in Year 6. If there are 27 children in Red class ($r$), how many children are in Blue class ($b$)?

There are 12 eggs in a carton ($c$). Sue buys 3 cartons and uses 8 eggs. How many eggs does Sue have left ($e$)?

## Think about ...

You can express each of the scenarios differently. There is no one correct expression.

For the 'What if?' question, try to think of a range of different contexts. You can change the letters $a$, $b$ and $c$ to other letters that have more relevance to your scenario.

## What if?

What might these algebraic equations be expressing?

Try to think of two different scenarios for each equation.

$9a = c$   $a - 10 = c$   $a + 12 = c$

$a + b = 24$   $2a - 20 = c$

When you've finished, turn to page 80.

# Wrapping your school

## Challenge

Christo is a famous artist who wraps up large buildings and open spaces with fabric.

What is the minimum amount of fabric that Christo would need to wrap up your school?

Write about how you arrived at your estimate. Include all your calculations.

**You will need:**
- measuring equipment

## Think about ...

Christo needs to wrap all the sides of your school and the roof as well. If your school has more than one building, he might need to wrap them up separately.

There may be some measurements that are not possible to take, so you will have to estimate what these are. Think carefully about the best way of making these estimates to ensure that your measurements are as accurate as possible.

## What if?

Christo doesn't only wrap up buildings. He and his wife Jeanne-Claude have wrapped up walkways, bridges and coastlines. They have even surrounded islands with fabric and created fabric paths on the surface of the water.

Estimate the minimum amount of fabric that Christo would need to cover different outdoor spaces in your school. These might be a playground, sports field or some other space.

Write about how you arrived at your estimates, including all your calculations.

When you've finished, turn to page 80.

# Redesigning your school

## Challenge

Imagine your school has been completely demolished.

Redesign your school so that it is improved for everyone who uses it.

Draw to scale a plan of your new school, including measurements.

**You will need:**
- squared paper
- ruler
- coloured pencils

## Think about ...

Think about the number of classrooms you need and all of the other different facilities your school requires.

Don't forget that your new school must fit on the current site.

## What if?

Try to find out an approximate cost for building your new school. What is included in this price? What's not included?

When you've finished, turn to page 80.

# Flying to other planets

## Challenge

If it takes a rocket one day to travel 500 000 kilometres, how long would it take to travel to the other planets in our solar system?

Write about how you worked out your answers.

| Planet | Approximate distance from Earth (km) |
|--------|--------------------------------------|
| Venus | 41 million |
| Mars | 78 million |
| Mercury | 92 million |
| Jupiter | 630 million |
| Saturn | 1276 million |
| Uranus | 2724 million |
| Neptune | 4350 million |

## Think about ...

Think about how far a rocket can travel in two days. What about 10 and 100 days?

For the 'What if?' question, you will need to do some rounding – think carefully as to whether you need to round up or down.

## What if?

If you were able to travel in a rocket that travels 500 000 kilometres per day, how old would you be when you landed on each of the planets if you set off on your next birthday?

Give your answers in years and months.

Write about how you worked out your answers.

When you've finished, turn to page 80.

# Ideal bedroom

## Challenge

Draw to scale a floor plan of your ideal bedroom.

Include all the furniture, drawn to scale.

Write all the dimensions on your plan, including the furniture.

Don't forget windows and doors.

**You will need:**
- furniture catalogue
- squared paper
- ruler

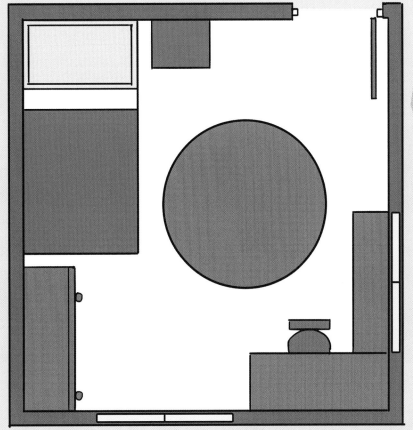

## Think about ...

Your ideal bedroom cannot be any more than 4 m by 3 m.

For the 'What if?', don't forget about paint, wallpaper and the cost of flooring.

## What if?

Investigate the cost of decorating your ideal bedroom, including the cost of all the furniture.

When you've finished, turn to page 80.

# Cost per kilometre

## Challenge

Choose ten places around the world and find the cheapest airfare to each of these destinations.

**You will need:**
- travel section from a newspaper
- atlas

Now find out how many kilometres it is to each of these destinations.

Calculate how much it would cost you to fly each kilometre to each of these destinations.

Show all your working out.

## Think about ...

You will probably need to round the cost of some of the airfares and the distances.

Depending on your destinations, it might be easier to make your calculations and comparisons based on the cost per 10 or 100 kilometres.

## What if?

Is there a big difference in the cost per kilometre to different destinations? If so, why do you think this is?

Which of your destinations offers the 'best value for money'?

Which destination offers the 'worst value for money'?

When you've finished, turn to page 80.

# Making playdough

## Challenge

In the USA, to save people weighing ingredients, recipes often use cupfuls rather than grams or millilitres.

Convert the recipe for playdough into an American one, replacing grams and millilitres with whole or part cupfuls.

### Things you need to know

One US cup is approximately the same as:

125 g of flour

240 ml of liquid

### Playdough

**You will need:**
• recipe book

250 g plain flour

50 g salt

about 120 ml water

1 to 2 tablespoons of cooking oil

few drops of food colouring (optional)

- Mix together the flour and salt in a large mixing bowl.
- Add the water and oil.
- Knead well until mixture is smooth. (You might need to add a bit more flour or water until the consistency is smooth but not sticky.)
- Add food colouring and knead until the colour is fully blended.
- Store in a plastic bag in the refrigerator until chilled enough to use.

## Think about ...

What is the ratio of flour to salt?

In most American cookbooks, cupfuls less than 1 cup are written as $\frac{3}{4}$ cup, $\frac{2}{3}$ cup, $\frac{1}{2}$ cup, $\frac{1}{3}$ cup or $\frac{1}{4}$ cup.

## What if?

Find a recipe that gives measurements in grams and millilitres and convert the recipe into an American one.

Cake or scone recipes are good ones to try.

When you've finished, turn to page 80.

# Greatest volume

## Challenge

Cut out several 10 units by 10 units squares.

Using scissors and sticky tape, make them into different-sized open boxes.

You will need to cut away the corners each time.

Which of your boxes has the greatest volume?

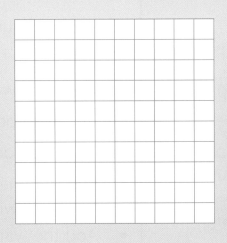

**You will need:**
- squared paper
- scissors
- sticky tape
- 3 pieces of card, all the same size
- small uniform lightweight substance for measuring capacity

 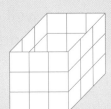

## Think about ...

How are you going to compare the capacity of your different-sized boxes?

What will happen if you make another box, with more/less cut from each corner?

Which box holds most? How do you know?

## What if?

Make three identical pieces of card into a cuboid, a triangular prism and a cylinder. All three shapes should be open at both ends.

Which shape do you think has the greatest volume, or will they all be the same?

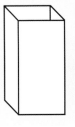 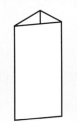 

When you've finished, turn to page 80.

# Earning interest

## Challenge

Investigate the best rate of interest you could earn if you had £100 to invest.

If you left the money there for 5 years, including interest, how much money would you have at the end of 5 years?

Show all your working out.

**You will need:**
• financial section from a newspaper and/or the internet

## Think about ...

The interest rate you are looking for is for saving money not borrowing money.

Choose interest rates where the interest is paid annually. Also, don't choose an interest rate that's a half, quarter or another fraction of a percent, for example 1·5% or 1·25%. Only choose whole percentages, such as 2%.

Remember that each time you are paid interest, it will start earning interest as well.

Round the amount of money you have at the end of each year to the nearest pound.

## What if?

What if you invested a **different** amount of money at the **same** interest rate but for a **different** number of years? How much money would you have at the end of the investment period?

Show all your working out.

When you've finished, turn to page 80.

# Property prices

## Challenge

What is the cost of an average home in your local area?

How does this compare with the cost of an average home in other parts of the country?

Write a report about the difference in property prices between your area and other parts of the country.

**You will need:**
• property section from newspapers

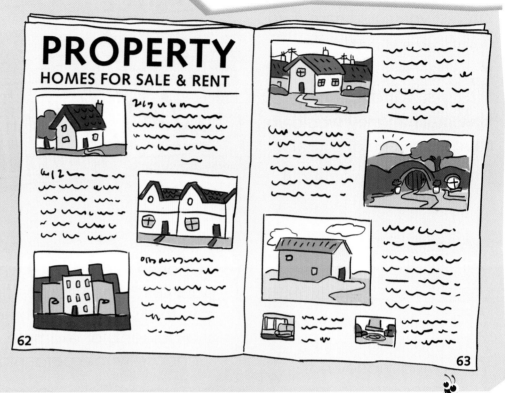

## Think about ...

What is meant by an 'average home'? In your area, does this mean a house or a flat? Does it mean a home with two or three bedrooms? Decide for yourself what is meant by an 'average home' in your local area.

In your report, try to use percentages to describe the differences in property prices.

## What if?

Is there a big difference in the cost of the average house compared with the cost of the average flat in your local area?

When you've finished, turn to page 80.

# Living expenses

## Challenge

The term 'cost of living' refers to the average amount of money that people in a particular place need in order to be able to afford basic food, housing, clothing and other everyday items.

Investigate how much money a family of five – two adults and three children – needs to live for a month.

Make sure you account for all the expenses.

**You will need:**
- household bills

## Think about ...

Think about:
- rent/mortgage
- gas
- electricity
- water
- telephone
- food
- car
- other expenses.

Different expenses occur at different times throughout the year. Some occur daily or weekly, while others occur monthly or even annually. You might need to multiply or divide to work out the cost per month. You might also need to make some estimations and approximations.

## What if?

Look at all the expenses you have used to calculate how much money a family of five needs to live for a month.

Place these expenses in order, starting with the greatest expense.

What is the greatest expense as a percentage of the overall monthly costs?

When you've finished, turn to page 80.

# Cost of light

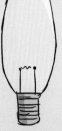

## Challenge

Using energy saving light bulbs can have a dramatic effect on how much electricity you use.

The table on the right compares the running cost of a standard bulb to an energy saving bulb.

Multiply the costs in the table by the number of lights in your home to work out how much is spent on lights per day and per year in your home.

Show your data collection and all the calculations you make, including your working out.

| Type of bulb | Power | Cost per day | Cost per year |
|---|---|---|---|
| Standard | 40 W | 2.77p | £10.12 |
| Energy Saving | 8 W | 0.55p | £2.02 |
| Standard | 60 W | 4.16p | £15.19 |
| Energy Saving | 11 W | 0.76p | £2.78 |
| Standard | 75 W | 5.20p | £18.98 |
| Energy Saving | 15 W | 1.04p | £3.80 |
| Standard | 100 W | 6.93p | £25.31 |
| Energy Saving | 18 W | 1.25p | £4.56 |

## Think about ...

The table above shows, for example, that a 40W standard bulb gives out the same amount of light as an 8W energy saving bulb, and a 100W standard bulb gives out the same amount of light as an 18W energy saving bulb.

You will need to find out the number of each type of light bulb you have in your home.

You might need to make some approximations.

## What if?

What would be the savings per week of using energy saving light bulbs as opposed to standard light bulbs?

What about over the course of a year?

Show all the calculations you make, including your working out.

When you've finished, turn to page 80.

# Going organic

## Challenge

Investigate the difference in the price of organic food compared to similar products in your local supermarket.

What generalisations can you make about any differences in prices?

**You will need:**
- prices for different food items

## Think about ...

Be sure to compare products that are as similar as possible and contain the same quantity.

Compare a range of products, including fruit and vegetables, meat and packaged foods.

## What if?

Investigate the difference in the price of fair trade food compared to similar products.

What generalisations can you make?

When you've finished, turn to page 80.

# Shape patterns

Using and applying mathematics in real-world contexts

## Challenge

- Trace around a large circular shape.
- Using a circular protractor, make intervals every 10°.
- Number the points 1 to 36.
- Using a 'multiply by 3' rule, join 1 to 3, 2 to 6, 3 to 9, and so on.
- Investigate what other patterns you can make using a 'multiply by 4' rule, that is: join 1 to 4, 2 to 8, 3 to 12 and so on.
- What about using a 'multiply by 6' rule, that is: join 1 to 6, 2 to 12, 3 to 18 and so on?
- What if you use a 'multiply by 2' rule, that is: join 1 to 2, 2 to 4, 3 to 6 and so on?

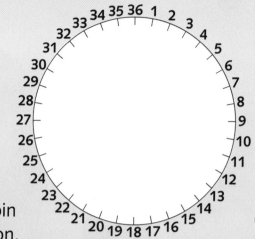

**You will need:**
- large circular shape
- circular protractor
- ruler
- coloured pencils (optional)
- squared paper

## Think about ...

You can either use a different circle for each circular pattern, or you can create all four patterns on the same large circle using four different colours.

## What if?

Draw an equilateral triangle with sides 13 cm.

Make 1 cm intervals on all three sides of the triangle.

What different patterns can you make by drawing lines between various intervals on the three sides of the triangle?

Investigate what patterns you can make using other shapes such as regular hexagons, pentagons and octagons.

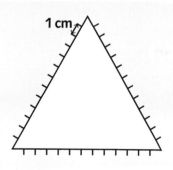

1 cm

When you've finished, turn to page 80.

# Coordinates patterns

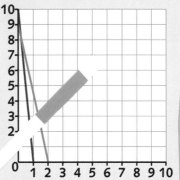

## Challenge

Use either a first quadrant coordinates grid with vertical and horizontal axes marked to 10, or use squared paper to draw and label a grid as shown on the right.

Join 1 to 10, 2 to 9, 3 to 8 and so on.

What if the grid is numbered like the one below?

Investigate what other patterns like this you can make on a first quadrant coordinates grid.

What if you use coloured pencils to shade different sections of your pattern? Make sure, however, that your coloured pattern has symmetry.

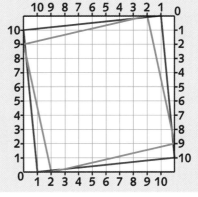

### You will need:

- first quadrant coordinates grid (vertical and horizontal axes marked to 10)
- four quadrant coordinates grid (vertical and horizontal axes marked to ± 10)
- squared paper (optional)
- coloured pencils
- ruler

## Think about ...

Take care to draw each line accurately.

Your coloured patterns could have vertical, horizontal or diagonal symmetry. Your patterns could even have more than one line of symmetry.

## What if?

Use either a four quadrant coordinates grid with vertical and horizontal axes marked to ± 10, or use squared paper to draw and label a grid as shown on the right.

Join (1, 0) to (0, 10); (1, 0) to (0, –10); (–1, 0) to (0, 10); (–1, 0) to (0, –10).

Join (2, 0) to (0, 9); (2, 0) to (0, –9); (–2, 0) to (0, 9); (–2, 0) to (0, –9).

Join (3, 0) to (0, 8); (3, 0) to (0, –8); (–3, 0) to (0, 8); (–3, 0) to (0, –8).

Continue the pattern.

What other patterns can you make using a four quadrant coordinates grid?

Think about using coloured pencils to shade different sections of your pattern, making sure that your coloured pattern has symmetry.

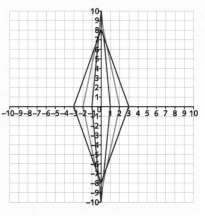

When you've finished, turn to page 80.

77

# Different languages

## Challenge

Look at the first 200 words of a book written in English.

Look at the first 200 words of a book written in another language.

Investigate the frequency with which different letters of the alphabet occur in different languages.

What conclusions can you make?

**You will need:**
- book/novel written in English
- books/novels written in other languages

## Think about ...

*How are you going to keep a record of the frequency of each letter?*

*The English language is based on the Latin (or Roman) alphabet. Choose books that are also based on the Latin alphabet.*

*Make sure that you don't choose a language that has too many letters.*

## What if?

In international Morse code, each letter of the alphabet is represented by a sequence of 'dots' and 'dashes'.

What are the Morse code sequences for the other letters of the alphabet?

Investigate the relationship between the number of dots and dashes used for different letters in Morse code and the frequency with which the letters are used.

As a rule, do the vowels have fewer dots and dashes than the consonants?

Investigate the Morse code sequences for the digits 0 to 9.

What patterns do you notice?

When you've finished, turn to page 80.

# Top 5 books

## Challenge

What are the five favourite books in your class?

Display your results.

Write about how you collected, organised and presented the data.

**You will need:**
- squared or graph paper
- ruler

## Think about ...

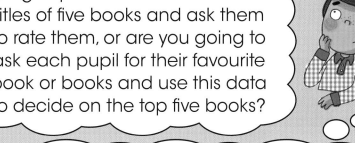

Think carefully about how you're going to collect the data. Are you going to present the class with the titles of five books and ask them to rate them, or are you going to ask each pupil for their favourite book or books and use this data to decide on the top five books?

For the 'What if?' task, think carefully about the most efficient way of collecting the data. Also, make sure that the way you collect the data from other classes/year groups means that you will be able to compare results between classes, including the results from your class.

How are you going to display your results? The way you collect your data will influence the way in which you display your results.

## What if?

The top five books for other classes/year groups in the school are likely to be different from your class. Why do you think this is?

Investigate the top five books for other classes/year groups in your school.

What comparisons can you make about the top five books for the different classes/year groups in your school?

When you've finished, turn to page 80.

**Share** Share your results.

**Discuss** Discuss any results that are different.

Which result is correct?

Might there be more than one solution?

 **Share** Share the methods used.

**Discuss** Discuss the similarities and differences in the methods used.

Which method worked best?

Are there any other ways to go about solving the problem?

 **Share** Share what you have learned.

**Discuss** Discuss what you would do the same, and what you would do differently next time.

Is there anything you would do differently?

What have you learned for next time?

What would you do the same?